AARON RODGERS

Champion Football Star

David Aretha

Enslow Publishing
101 W. 23rd Street
Suite 240
New York, NY 10011
USA

enslow.com

Published in 2018 by Enslow Publishing, LLC.
101 W. 23rd Street, Suite 240, New York, NY 10011

Library of Congress Cataloging-in-Publication Data

Names: Aretha, David, author.
Title: Aaron Rodgers : champion football star / David Aretha.
Description: New York : Enslow Publishing, 2018. | Series: Sports Star
  Champions | Includes bibliographical references and index. | Audience:
  Grade 6-8.
Identifiers: LCCN 2017003130| ISBN 9780766087163 (library-bound) | ISBN
  9780766087514 (pbk.) | ISBN 9780766087521 (6-pack)
Subjects: LCSH: Rodgers, Aaron, 1983- —Juvenile literature. | Football
  players—United States—Biography—Juvenile literature. | Quarterbacks
  (Football)—United States—Biography—Juvenile literature.
Classification: LCC GV939.R6235 A74 2018 | DDC 796.332092 [B] —dc23
LC record available at https://lccn.loc.gov/2017003130

Printed in the United States of America

To Our Readers: We have done our best to make sure all websites in this book were active and appropriate when we went to press. However, the author and the publisher have no control over and assume no liability for the material available on those websites or on any websites they may link to. Any comments or suggestions can be sent by e-mail to customerservice@enslow.com.

Contents

Introduction:
Miracle in Motown

Aaron Rodgers had overcome the odds before. But on this Thursday night at Ford Field in Detroit, he would need a miracle.

It was December 3, 2015, with the Green Bay Packers (7–4) battling the Lions (4–7) in Detroit's indoor stadium. With 23 seconds remaining, the Packers trailed 23–21 and were in desperate straits. They had the ball on their 21-yard-line with no timeouts.

Rodgers, the bearded, droopy-eyed superstar, remained calm and confident. He had orchestrated many comebacks in his eleven years with Green Bay, although nothing like this. His first pass fell incomplete. So did his second. Now he was in a seemingly impossible situation, with six seconds left and 79 yards from the goal line.

Packers coach Mike McCarthy called for the hook-and-ladder play. Before the snap, CBS announcer Jim Nantz called it an "absolute desperation moment." Rodgers fired the ball 16 yards to wide receiver James Jones, who pitched it back to tight end Richard Rodgers. *That* Rodgers, facing tacklers, threw the ball way back to Aaron Rodgers at the 24. The quarterback was immediately tackled. Game over … or was it?

A referee ruled that Detroit's Devin Taylor had grabbed Rodgers's facemask, resulting in a 15-yard penalty. Replays showed that Taylor had barely touched the facemask, but no matter: The play stood. The clock read 0:00, but since a game can't end on a penalty, Green Bay had one more play.

The Packers had the ball on their 39-yard line, and McCarthy called for the "Hail Mary" play—a long chuck into the end zone.

Rodgers posted a 90–45 record as a starter from 2008 through 2016—including the mind-blowing triumph in Detroit on December 3, 2015.

Many Hail Marys had been completed in National Football League (NFL) history, but few were as lengthy as this.

Rodgers dropped back to pass and faced a heavy rush. To avoid a sack, he scrambled back to the 22. Then he found daylight on the right side. He ran past the 30 and took a couple of steps forward to gain momentum. Then, from the 36, he launched the ball like an Olympic

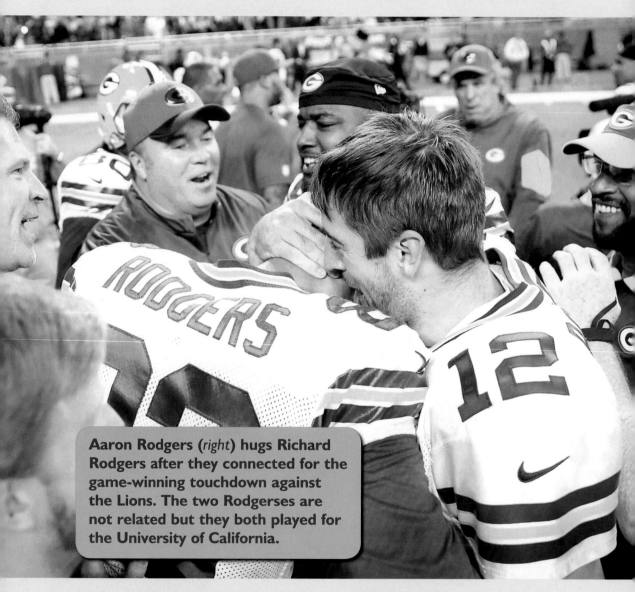

Aaron Rodgers (*right*) hugs Richard Rodgers after they connected for the game-winning touchdown against the Lions. The two Rodgerses are not related but they both played for the University of California.

javelin thrower. He rainbowed the ball so high that "I thought it was going to hit the ceiling," said teammate B. J. Raji.

The ball traveled 61 yards and stayed in the air for 5.42 seconds. Finally, it descended into the end zone. A crowd of five Lions and four Packers—heads craning upward—converged on the falling bomb. The man in front of the pack, six-foot-four Richard Rodgers, jumped high and grabbed it with both hands. "A leaping touchdown catch is made," screamed Green Bay radio announcer Wayne Larrivee, "and the Packers have won! … An unbe*liev*able finish!"

"I've never had a completed Hail Mary before," Aaron said afterward. Forevermore, the play would be called the "Miracle in Motown."

Incredibly, Rodgers would complete another Hail Mary pass a month later in the NFL playoffs. These were just two of the many spectacular moments in Rodgers's illustrious career. Five years earlier, he had led Green Bay to a Super Bowl title. Twice he had won the league's MVP Award. In addition, his passer rating, which ranks quarterbacks, had been the highest in NFL history.

And to think, when Rodgers had been a high school player, not a single Division I college had offered him a scholarship. Nobody wanted him. But, as he would on that Thursday night in Detroit, Aaron Rodgers overcame the odds.

The QB Nobody Wanted

One day in a parent-teacher conference, Darla Rodgers received some bizarre news about her kindergartner, little Aaron Rodgers. Bette Lawler, Aaron's teacher in Chico, California, remembers the story.

"I told her that Aaron was so nice to everyone and really well behaved," Lawler said. "But I wanted her to know just how much time he spent drawing up football plays."

That's right, Aaron was playing quarterback at the age of six. According to his teacher, he was "drawing these little circles and Xs and lines" in class prior to recess. Apparently, that's when the big football games took place.

Aaron Charles Rodgers, who arrived in the world on December 2, 1983, had athleticism in his genes. His father,

Aaron's hometown of Chico, California (*pictured*), feels like a world away from Green Bay, Wisconsin. In Chico, the average high temperature in February is 61 degrees. In Green Bay, it's 28.

Ed, had been an offensive lineman in college before eventually becoming a chiropractor. His mother had been a dancer. Together, they raised three boys in Chico, a pleasant Northern California town known as the "City of Trees." Older brother Luke, Aaron's sports buddy, was nineteen months older. Jordan would arrive five years after Aaron.

Early on, Aaron showed an intense interest in football. At age two, he would sit on the couch and watch an entire NFL game without fussing. He became a huge fan of the San Francisco 49ers, who, in 1989, used two quarterbacks—Joe Montana and Steve Young—to storm to the Super Bowl. Aaron watched in delight as his team crushed Denver 55–10 on Super Bowl Sunday. Little did Aaron know that he would someday join Montana and Young in the ranks of the greatest quarterbacks of all time.

By age five, Aaron could recognize offensive plays that the 49ers ran—something most adult fans can't do. All the while he practiced throwing footballs through a tire that hung from a tree. "That's when I began thinking his mind was really amazing and his physical attributes were phenomenal," said family friend Larry Ruby.

Aaron continued to display physical, visual, and mental acumen on the field of play. His father shot film of him in second grade dribbling a basketball with both hands and dishing no-look passes. No matter the ball, Aaron could throw it hard and accurately. As a Little League pitcher, he rifled fastballs that belied his modest size.

Aaron was normally modest and gentlemanly, but when it came to sports, confidence surged within him. During an admittance interview with Champion Christian, where he attended eighth grade, the principal said, "Tell me one thing

"I never worried about him breaking a window because he was always so darn accurate."
—Liane Christensen, who watched Aaron throw the football around the yard with her sons

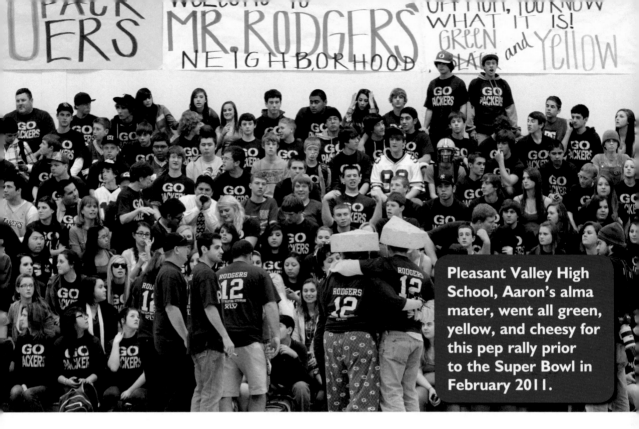

Pleasant Valley High School, Aaron's alma mater, went all green, yellow, and cheesy for this pep rally prior to the Super Bowl in February 2011.

you can do to make the school better." Aaron replied, "Your sports teams are going to be really good."

Luke and Aaron became consumed with sports, playing one-on-one basketball into the night. Aaron's size, though, was a shortcoming. Entering Pleasant Valley High School, he stood only five-foot-eight and weighed around 135 pounds. But he continued to fill out—to six-foot-one, 185 pounds as a senior—and started at quarterback his last two seasons.

Aaron threw for more than 2,000 yards as a junior, and he set the school single-season passing record as a senior (2,303 yards). He looked like a future college QB. College recruiters, though, didn't make the long drive to Chico to see him. In that pre-internet era, the only way for college coaches to see film footage of Aaron was if his high school coaches mailed them videotapes. They sent out some but not enough. Not a single Division I university offered him a scholarship.

In December 2001, his senior year, Aaron thought about giving up on football. Then along came Craig Rigsbee, the coach at nearby Butte College. The friendly coach convinced Aaron to use Butte as a stepping-stone. After shining on the gridiron for the Roadrunners, he would attract Division I offers. "I was kind of down and out about the whole thing, but he gave me my dreams back," Aaron has said.

UP CLOSE

Talent plus hard work equals success. Aaron Rodgers is living proof.

"When I was in high school, they'd have a list of the top 100 quarterbacks in the state. And I wasn't on there," he said. "And I was ticked. So I said I'm going to work out twice."

First he'd work out in the morning, "then I'm going to go to class, then work out again because I know—*I know*—those kids in the top 100? They aren't doing that."

A slender, clean-shaven Rodgers threw nineteen touchdown passes and just five interceptions in his first season as Cal's quarterback.

In 2002, he threw for 2,408 yards, 28 touchdowns, and just four interceptions. He led Butte to a No. 2 national ranking among junior colleges and earned junior college All-American honors. Just as Rigsbee had predicted, the big schools became interested. University of California at Berkeley head coach Jeff Tedford attended a practice and was impressed with the young man's composure and leadership.

The following year, Aaron enrolled at Cal-Berkeley, also known simply as Cal. On the field, he played like a seasoned veteran. He won the starting job in the fifth game of the season and finished the year with 2,903 passing yards, 19 touchdowns, and just five interceptions. Five times he threw for 300 or more yards, tying a school record. In the Insight Bowl, he burned Virginia Tech for 394 aerial yards in a 52–49 victory. Though unknown to the world in August, Aaron had suddenly become a star.

In 2004, Aaron led Cal to a 10–1 regular season record—the team's best mark in 54 years. He amassed 2,566 passing yards, 24 touchdowns, and eight interceptions. After a 41–6 rout of rival Stanford on November 20, adoring fans raised him in the air and chanted, "One more year! One more year!" They wanted him to return to Cal for his senior season. But Aaron, the First Team All-Pac-10 quarterback in 2004, decided to turn pro instead—with good reason. Prior to the 2005 NFL Draft, some experts predicted that Aaron would be the first player chosen in the first round. And who had that No. 1 pick? The team he had rooted for since his toddler days in Chico—the San Francisco 49ers.

2

Northern Star

Prior to the 2005 NFL Draft, teams praised Rodgers for his accurate arm and athleticism. Other than that, they had many concerns. NFL scouts, according to the *Milwaukee Journal Sentinel*, said:

"He's a little short."

"There are some things that are just ordinary about him."

"He gets sacked a lot."

"He's mechanically very rigid."

"Can't create on his own."

"Panics under pressure."

"Gets flustered easy."

"I don't like him."

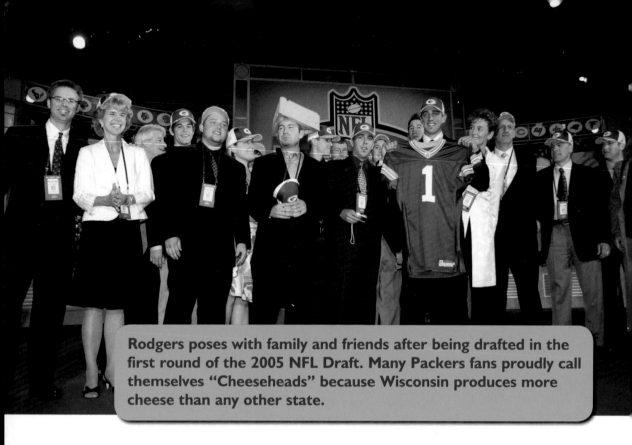

Rodgers poses with family and friends after being drafted in the first round of the 2005 NFL Draft. Many Packers fans proudly call themselves "Cheeseheads" because Wisconsin produces more cheese than any other state.

Still, for a while, some predicted that the 49ers would draft Rodgers with the top overall pick. San Francisco desperately needed a quarterback, and he and Alex Smith of the University of Utah were considered the two best.

At the NFL Draft in New York City that April, the 49ers chose Smith. After that initial selection, Rodgers waited all the way to the 23rd pick before the Green Bay Packers called his name. Years later, he would say it was good that he had dropped that low in the first round. "I was 21 years old [and] I thought I was the best thing since sliced bread, and I needed a little humble pie."

The California kid would play in the NFL's coldest city, 1,750 miles away from home. When he first arrived in Green Bay, there was snow on the ground—in late April. "Man, where the heck am I?" he wondered.

Still, Rodgers said, "I'm excited about going to Green Bay and being able to learn from the greatest quarterback in the league right now." That QB was fourteen-year veteran Brett Favre, considered a "god" in Wisconsin. Favre, a warrior and gunslinger, had twice led Green Bay to the Super Bowl, winning once.

Financially, Rodgers's life improved dramatically. He signed a five-year contract worth at least $5.4 million, with the option of earning much more if he became a starter. Prior to training camp in 2005, he bought a large house in a Green Bay suburb, which he filled with furniture from Pier 1. Then he hunkered down and set about learning the team's playbook, throwing "a couple hundred balls a day" to his brother Luke.

For his first three NFL seasons, Rodgers served as backup to legendary Packers quarterback Brett Favre (*left*). He played in only seven games and started none.

Rodgers was anything but an overnight success. In his first preseason game, he completed only two of his first seven passes and was sacked twice. The Packers suffered through a 4–12 season in 2005, and Rodgers played in just three games during "garbage" time. He completed nine passes in 16 attempts. Each week in practice, though, he played extremely hard. Wide receiver Donald Driver said that Rodgers played each practice possession "like it was the last possession of his life."

After the 2005 season, Mike McCarthy became Green Bay's new head coach. He required Rodgers to attend his "quarterback school." There, Rodgers worked on his throwing mechanics, hand-eye coordination, and conditioning. It was grueling, and he didn't like it. "I fought the system," he said. "Change has always been tough. Any type of change in my life I've always met with some resistance." He and the coach butted heads over the course of that first year.

All that hard work made Rodgers a better player. Yet the question remained: Would he ever play? Favre kept postponing his retirement, remaining the starter through 2007.

"The more prepared I can be each week, the less pressure I feel and the more confident I am."
—Aaron Rodgers

Rodgers played in just two games in 2006, breaking his foot in one of them. He entered only two games in 2007 as well, though he shined in a matchup with Dallas. Coming in for an injured Favre against the Cowboys, Rodgers completed 18 of 26 passes for 201 yards and a touchdown.

In March 2008, the Packers traded Favre, meaning Rodgers would be their starting quarterback. When he heard the news, he remained California cool. "I was excited," he said. "But to be honest, it was just another day. I had plans to play golf and see my buddy in LA, and that's pretty much what I did."

In the season opener at Green Bay's Lambeau Field, which was a Monday Night Football broadcast, Rodgers enjoyed "running out of the tunnel to the electric atmosphere we had." He threw with pinpoint accuracy, completing 18 of 22 passes in a win over Minnesota. After running for a touchdown in the fourth quarter, he jumped into the arms of fans in the

Aaron pinpoints a pass against Dallas on November 29, 2007. This was the first time he got to play significant minutes, and he completed 69 percent of his 26 passes.

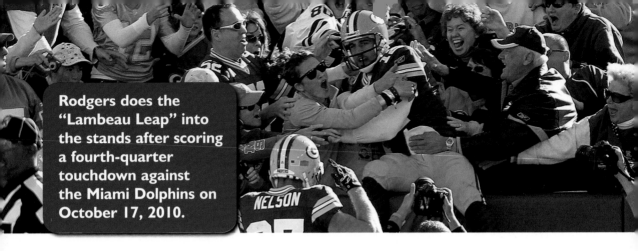

Rodgers does the "Lambeau Leap" into the stands after scoring a fourth-quarter touchdown against the Miami Dolphins on October 17, 2010.

stands—a tradition called the "Lambeau Leap." "I've been dreaming about that for four years, to be honest," he said.

The Packers won just six of Rodgers's sixteen starts in 2008, but they couldn't blame the quarterback. Rodgers led an offense that ranked fifth in the NFL in points scored. He threw for 4,038 yards and 28 touchdowns, both of which ranked fourth in the league.

In 2009, Rodgers emerged as a genuine star. He was named National Football Conference (NFC) Player of the Month for October after completing 75 percent of his passes while averaging 329 yards per game. Twice during the season he topped 380 yards in a game, and he led Green Bay to an 11–5 record.

Favre had been the face of the Packers for sixteen years. But, the *New York Times* proclaimed during the 2009 season, "The Packers are Aaron Rodgers's team now." His No. 12 jersey became the biggest-selling Packers shirt.

Rodgers's incredible focus, first displayed as a small boy, was manifesting in the pros. In 2009, he again ranked fourth in the NFL in passing yards (4,434) and touchdown tosses (30). All the while, he had the lowest interception rate in the league at 1.3 percent. Thus began a yearly trend for Rodgers—huge yardage and TD numbers, and very few interceptions. That year, Packers running back Ahman Green called Rodgers a "cool customer." "This guy," added wide receiver Greg Jennings, "could be the MVP of the NFL right now."

In the first round of the playoffs that year, Rodgers threw for 423 yards against Arizona. However, his season ended in overtime that day on a devastating play. A Cardinals defender sacked him, forcing a fumble that was returned for a touchdown. Rodgers slammed his helmet to the ground in disgust.

To become a championship-level quarterback, Rodgers knew he had to take his game to an even higher level.

UP CLOSE

At the end of the 2009 season, Rodgers was named to the Pro Bowl, the NFL's "all-star game," played at Aloha Stadium in Honolulu, Hawaii. Aaron threw two touchdown passes that day, including a 48-yarder to Steve Smith. He was named to the Pro Bowl again in 2011, '12, '14, '15, and '16.

3

Super Bowl Champ and MVP

Entering the 2010 season, the Packers had the talent to go all the way. "Super Bowl or die!" proclaimed linebacker Nick Barnett in training camp.

Relentless linebacker Clay Matthews, with his long blond hair, keyed a powerful defense. Rodgers, now one of the NFL's elite quarterbacks, led a high-scoring offense. Unfortunately, numerous injuries weakened the team. Rodgers himself missed a game and a half with a concussion. Green Bay lost six games on the season, all of them by seven points or less. Although the Packers made the playoffs as a wildcard team, they would have to win three postseason games on the road to reach the Super Bowl.

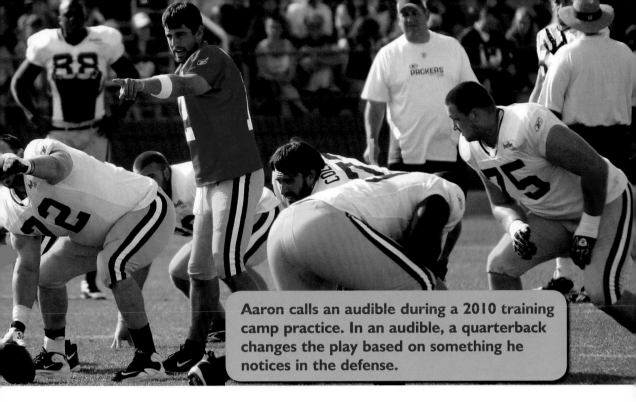

Aaron calls an audible during a 2010 training camp practice. In an audible, a quarterback changes the play based on something he notices in the defense.

Nevertheless, Mike McCarthy's team believed in themselves. Said NFL Films producer Dave Douglas, "Once they got in the playoffs, I think they said ... so we have to play four games away from Lambeau? Big deal. We can do it. And they did it."

First, the Packers ventured to Philadelphia and slayed the Eagles 21–16, with Rodgers throwing three touchdown passes. Next, they blew out Atlanta 48–21 as Rodgers completed 31 of 36 passes for 366 yards and three touchdowns. "This probably was my best performance—the stage we were on, the importance of this game," he said. "It was a good night."

In the NFC Championship Game, the Packers battled their archrival, the Bears, in Chicago. In bitter-cold temperatures,

Green Bay toughed out a 21–14 victory, thanks in part to Rodgers's "defense." In the third quarter, he threw an interception to Brian Urlacher at the Bears' five-yard-line. It looked like the superstar linebacker would return 95 yards for a touchdown. Rodgers, though, raced downfield and dove at his ankles. "He threw it to me—then he tackled me," Urlacher said.

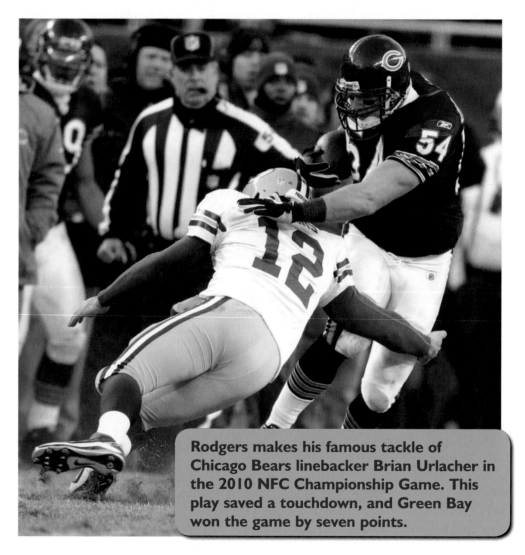

Rodgers makes his famous tackle of Chicago Bears linebacker Brian Urlacher in the 2010 NFC Championship Game. This play saved a touchdown, and Green Bay won the game by seven points.

Rodgers celebrates the Super Bowl win with Packers superstar linebacker Clay Matthews. Near the end of the game, fans chanted, "Aa-ron Rod-gers!" and "M-V-P!"

Next, Green Bay battled Pittsburgh in Super Bowl XLV in Dallas. Eight years earlier, few people outside of Northern California had ever heard of Aaron Rodgers. On Super Bowl Sunday, a TV audience of 111 million watched his every move.

Yet again, he remained California cool. In the first half, he threw a 29-yard touchdown pass to Jordy Nelson and a 21-yard TD toss to Greg Jennings. Green Bay led 21–3 in the second quarter, but the Steelers eventually closed the gap to 21–17. With 12:03 left in the game, Rodgers connected with Jennings for an eight-yard touchdown, making the score 28–21. "It's a great day to be great, baby!" Jennings said.

Green Bay hung on to win 31–25. Rodgers, who had completed 24 of 39 passes for 304 yards, three touchdowns, and no interceptions, was named Super Bowl MVP. "With Aaron

Rodgers, we put this game on his shoulders," McCarthy said. "He delivered."

Rodgers's life changed after his Super Bowl win. He was bombarded with requests for interviews, appearances, and product endorsements. The following summer, the champion Packers traveled to the White House to meet President Barack Obama. As a former Chicago resident, Obama wanted Rodgers on his hometown team. "I think we should initiate a trade to send Rodgers down to the Bears," he told the Packers. "What do you think?" They laughed and booed. Rodgers responded by presenting the president with a Packers jersey. "All right, man," Obama said. "Thank you."

> **"I knew Aaron had a special gift, but you never think your kid is going to wind up at the highest level possible."**
> —Ed Rodgers

Rodgers was garnering so much respect in 2011 that rookies in training camp were referring to him as "sir." He told his mom, "I feel like I'm one of the older guys now. And I'm only 27."

That year, Rodgers approached quarterback perfection. Despite a mediocre defense, Green Bay opened the season at 13–0. The Packers would go on to score 560 points, the third-highest point total in NFL history (since 1990). Against

Denver, Rodgers threw for 408 yards. In back-to-back games against Minnesota and San Diego, he completed 80 percent of his passes. Five times he threw at least four touchdowns in a game, including five in the season finale against the Bears.

"Right now, Aaron Rodgers is the best player in the game," said former NFL quarterback Phil Simms.

"Aaron is definitely the best at throwing the deep ball that I've had the opportunity to work with," said McCarthy.

Even Hall of Fame quarterback Steve Young, one of Rodgers's idols as a kid, gushed about the Packers superstar. "Tom [Brady] and Peyton [Manning] are the quarterback gold standard," Young said. "The difference is both guys need protection and are on the back side of brilliant careers. Aaron can go create with his legs if he has to. You almost can't defend Aaron."

In 2011, Rodgers set Packers season records for TD passes (45), passing yards (4,643), completion percentage (68.3), and 300-yard games (eight). His touchdown/interception ratio (45/6) was one of the best in history. His 8.22 yards per pass attempt were fifth most in history. More importantly, he helped Green Bay become the sixth NFL team ever to win fifteen games.

The 15–1, defending Super Bowl champion Packers entered their first playoff game as a huge favorite over

Though not known for his speed, Aaron has great field awareness and often runs for a first down. He has averaged around five yards per carry in his career.

UP CLOSE

In 2011, Rodgers set the NFL single-season record for passer rating with a mark of 122.5. Passer rating is a complicated formula that evaluates a player's passing attempts, completions, passing yards, passing touchdowns, and interceptions. Basically, a quarterback will have a high passer rating if he completes a high percentage of his passes, throws for a lot of yards and TDs, and avoids interceptions. Aaron's best passer rating game in 2011 occurred at Minnesota. He completed 24 of 30 passes for 335 yards, three touchdowns, and no interceptions.

the New York Giants. Stunningly, the Giants prevailed at Lambeau Field 37–20. The Packers had only themselves to blame. Green Bay fumbled away three balls, including one by Rodgers, and their receivers dropped multiple passes. The ferocious Giants defense pressured Rodgers all day, causing him to kick the dirt in frustration. "He looked a little out of sorts," Giants defensive end Justin Tuck said. "I wouldn't say rattled, but frustrated."

Following the playoffs, the Associated Press named Rodgers the 2011 NFL Most Valuable Player. He would have traded the award for another Super Bowl ring. "I have accomplished a lot individually," he said, "and now it's all about winning some more championships."

Up Close and Personal

4

Aaron Rodgers's eyes burn with anger. A house fly has landed on his coffee table, and now he's about to destroy it with a golf club. "No one," he growls to the fly, "comes into *this* house without paying the price." Rodgers swings mightily at the fly but loses his grip on the club, which smashes through his living room window and then into a car window. "Did you get it?" asks teammate Clay Matthews, sitting on the couch. Aaron just shrugs.

Rodgers looks stylish as he poses at the **ESPY Awards in Los Angeles in July 2016.** He has appeared on dozens of TV shows, including *Ellen, Jeopardy!,* and *The Tonight Show.*

Aaron sometimes says unexpected things to opposing players during the middle of a game. Here he shares a laugh with Chicago Bears cornerback Cre'Von LeBlanc.

This was the latest in a string of commercials Rodgers filmed for State Farm Insurance. Along with retired quarterback Peyton Manning, he may be the most entertaining athlete in TV advertising. His serious face, along with his dry sense of humor, frequently elicits smiles and laughs.

In 2015, the *Wall Street Journal* reported just how strange Rodgers's sense of humor can be. For example, during games, he'll sometimes make unexpected comments to opposing players. Tampa Bay linebacker Mason Foster said that after Rodgers had completed a long pass, he calmly asked him about his college team. "He just walks up and asks me how [the University of] Washington is doing," Foster said. "In between plays."

In the locker room, Rodgers's odd jokes are often met with blank looks. "His jokes are what we call 'Algebra 2,'" said former teammate Daryn Colledge. "I think a lot of people don't get it."

Often, Rodgers will quote from his favorite movie, *The Princess Bride*, a romantic comedy from 1987. His favorite line from the movie is, "Let me put it this way. Have you ever heard of Plato, Aristotle, Socrates? Morons."

Rodgers said he jokes around with young teammates to put them at ease—an important quality for a team leader. "He's about as relaxed and calm in this locker room as you can get," said Packers offensive tackle Bryan Bulaga. "His demeanor has an effect on us. There's never any panic in this locker room. Everything about him says, 'Take a breather; we are going to be all right.'"

"I'm not a lot of fun to be around when I'm not doing well at golf. We played Wiffle ball the other day, and I was ticked we lost at that. I don't like losing at video games."

—Aaron Rodgers

Rodgers is all smiles after the Packers defeated the Washington Redskins, 35–18, in a 2016 Wild Card Playoff game.

Teammates appreciate Rodgers's humble rise to stardom—how he had to prove himself in junior college after the larger schools had passed on him.

"We saw the path he's traveled to get to where he's gotten, and we respect that a whole heck of a lot," said Packers fullback John Kuhn. "Aaron can really relate to the guys on a personal level more so than probably most superstar athletes."

As of 2017, Rodgers remains a bachelor. He had been dating actress Olivia Munn for more than two years, first meeting her at a Country Music Awards event. On the TV show *Conan*, Munn recalled her initial conversation with the MVP and Super Bowl champion: "I said, 'So what do you do?' And he said, 'Oh, I play football.' 'Cool. What college?' And he's like, 'Oh, no. I play professional.' And I was like, 'Cool—what position?' 'Quarterback.' 'Cool.'"

UP CLOSE

In the offseason, Rodgers lives in a huge house in Del Mar, California, north of San Diego. The estate reportedly includes a swimming pool, basketball court, sports room, gym, spa, sauna, home cinema, and gaming room. It's elaborate, to be sure, but he insists he's just a regular guy. "I think some people forget sometimes I do have to go to the grocery store," he said in 2013. "I have to get my oil changed from time to time. I do all the normal things. I cut my grass."

A year before he met Munn, Rodgers signed a five-year contract with the Packers worth $110 million. Throughout his career, he has proven to be charitable with his money and time. He has contributed to numerous charities, including the Midwest Athletes Against Childhood Cancer (MACC) Fund. Since 2010, he has hosted the annual "Evening with Aaron Rodgers" in Milwaukee, Wisconsin, raising more than $2 million for MACC.

Rodgers has spent time with many courageous kids who have battled cancer. He recalled playing catch with a child named Dijon in the boy's backyard and jumping on a tram-

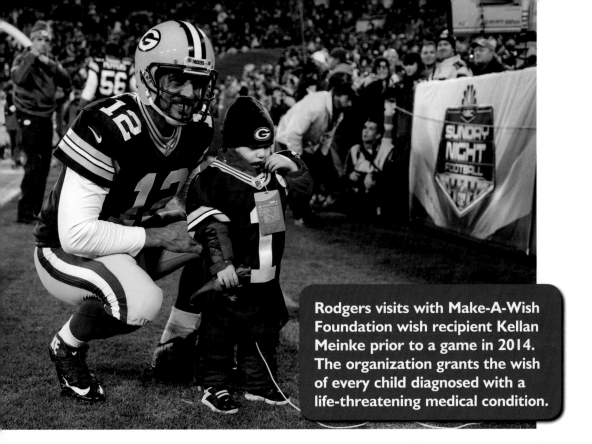

Rodgers visits with Make-A-Wish Foundation wish recipient Kellan Meinke prior to a game in 2014. The organization grants the wish of every child diagnosed with a life-threatening medical condition.

poline with a young girl named Maggie. "I try to remember the things that I see in their eyes, and their hearts," he said. "It gives you great perspective. It reminds you to really enjoy life because these kids have been through so much, and they have such joy for the opportunity to live, and to dream, and to have goals."

A longtime participant in the Make-A-Wish Foundation, Rodgers also has worked for The Salvation Army, IndependenceFirst, Raise Hope for Congo, and more.

The website itsAaron.com raises awareness for important causes that are not well publicized. One such cause is

Camp Hometown Heroes, which provides a weeklong camp outing for kids who have lost a loved one in service to the US military. He has said that the camps help kids talk about what they're going through and grieve, and they meet other kids who have gone through the same things they are experiencing.

In an emotionally moving video that has generated hundreds of thousands of views, Aaron hangs out with four such kids. Like he does with his Packer teammates, Rodgers is able to put the three sisters and a teenage boy, Dylan, at ease. He's relaxed, he smiles warmly, and he asks them lots of questions. Pretty soon, Dylan says, "I'm going to take a selfie with you. Because you're Aaron Rodgers, and no one at school will believe me if I told them."

While on a boat with Aaron, young Kylee, her brown hair in a ponytail, soon becomes his fishing pal. "There are these kids in my class that *love* football, and they are a fan of you," she says with an adoring smile.

"Really?" he says. "Are you not a fan of football?"

"Not really," she says, casually. "There's so much going on."

Like hanging out with Aaron Rodgers.

It was a day Dylan, Kylee, and her sisters would never forget.

5

Magic Man

Life was going smoothly for Rodgers until November 4, 2013, when the Bears' Shea McClellin slammed him to the turf. Early in that Thursday night game in Chicago, he lay writhing on the field with a fractured collarbone. Though the Packers had entered the game at 5–2, they fell to the Bears and their season was in jeopardy. That's what happens when you lose a quarterback as mighty as Aaron Rodgers.

The previous season had been a typical one for the superstar QB. He again paced the NFL in passer rating (108.0). He led Green Bay to an 11–5 record and the NFC North title. And he marshaled the Pack to a playoff victory over Minnesota before losing the next week to San Francisco.

UP CLOSE

What would Rodgers do if he weren't playing football? In 2011, he said he would have served in the military, adding that "my grandfather served proudly in World War II." In 2016, he speculated about his post-football career. "I'm a fan of documentaries, and to be able to be a part of a group that's bringing awareness to subjects that don't get a lot of attention at times [is appealing]. I enjoy the TV program *Vice*, because they tackle some really interesting issues. To be a part of something like that would be really interesting."

But for most of November and December 2013, Rodgers was confined to the sidelines. On Thanksgiving Day, he threw his clipboard on the ground in disgust while Detroit stuffed the Packers like a turkey, 40–10. The loss put them at 5–6–1, while Detroit sat atop the North Division standings at 7–5.

By late December, everything changed. The Lions were out of the race at 7–8, and on December 29, the Packers played in Chicago. The winner of that bitterly cold season-finale game would capture the division title. Rodgers, who hadn't played since the last Chicago game, made a triumphant return. He threw for 318 yards, including 48 of the most famous yards in Packers history.

Down 28–27 late in the game, the Packers twice converted a fourth-and-one to stay alive. Then, with 46 seconds remaining, they faced a fourth-and-eight at the Bears' 48. Rodgers endured a heavy rush, but he quickly escaped and rolled left. He then stopped, squared his body, and flicked a deep ball to a wide-open Randall Cobb. "It was in the air for so long," Cobb later said. "I had so many thoughts going through my head: 'You better not drop it. If you drop it they are going to kill you. Just catch the ball.'"

Cobb caught the ball at the 10 and stormed into the end zone for the winning score. That play, said Packers coach Mike McCarthy, "will be running on the highlights for the rest of my time on this earth. What a great finish!"

The jubilation, though, was short-lived. In the Packers' first playoff game, with the temperature close to zero in Green Bay, San Francisco kicked a field goal as time expired to prevail, 23–20.

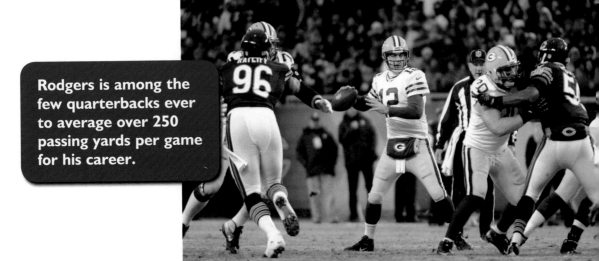

Rodgers is among the few quarterbacks ever to average over 250 passing yards per game for his career.

Rodgers leaves a game against Detroit with an injury on December 28, 2014. But, you can't keep this man down! Two weeks later, he led Green Bay to victory over Dallas in the playoffs.

Rodgers returned to dominant form in 2014. At one point, he threw 214 consecutive passes without an interception. On November 9, he became the second NFL QB ever to throw six touchdown passes in one half. He couldn't suppress his smiles as Green Bay led 42–0 at intermission. The Pack won 55–14, then whipped Philadelphia a week later, 53–20. In the season finale against Detroit, the winner would take the NFC North title. Rodgers again proved heroic. He left the game with a torn calf muscle, went to the locker room, and then limped back onto the field. The rest of the way, he completed 13 of 15 passes with two TDs; Green Bay won 30–20.

Rodgers finished the season with 38 TD passes and just five interceptions, earning his second NFL MVP Award. After an impressive playoff win over Dallas, the Packers journeyed to Seattle for the NFC Championship Game and suffered the most devastating loss in team history. With four minutes remaining, Green Bay led 19–7 and punted to Seattle. The

Seahawks scored a touchdown, recovered an onside kick, and scored another TD. A two-point conversion made it 22–19, and a Green Bay field goal at 0:14 tied it at 22. The Seahawks won in overtime on a 35-yard Russell Wilson touchdown pass. "It's going to be a missed opportunity that I'll probably think about for the rest of my career," Rodgers said. "We can't blame anybody but ourselves."

Rodgers entered 2015 with a career passer rating of 106.0, the best of any quarterback in NFL history. However, with Pro Bowl wide receiver Jordy Nelson injured all season, his 92.7 rating in that year was the lowest of his career. So, too, were his 60.7 percent completion percentage and 239 passing yards per game. The Packers snuck into the playoffs as a 10–6 wildcard team and beat Washington on the road.

The next week at Arizona, Rodgers nearly pulled off another miracle. Trailing 20–13 with 55 seconds left, Rodgers heaved a 60-yard completion to wide receiver

"The guys who stick around are the smartest guys and the guys who are the most self-driven. You have to have drive. The coaches can only take you so far. You have to want to learn and work."
—Aaron Rodgers

Despite his warm-weather roots, Rodgers has thrived in cold, snowy conditions in Green Bay. Here he trots off the field after a triumph over the Houston Texans in December 2016.

Jeff Janis. Then, with five seconds remaining, he completed a 41-yard Hail Mary to Janis for the touchdown. The game went to overtime, and the Cardinals won on an opening-drive TD.

In 2016, Rodgers continued to wow fans. With Green Bay struggling at 4–6, he announced that the Packers could "run the table"—that is, win their remaining games and make the playoffs. Incredibly, they did! His 60-yard pass to Jordy Nelson with seconds remaining helped Green Bay beat Chicago 30–27. The Pack won at Detroit in the season finale to win the division title. They then beat the Giants and the Cowboys in the playoffs. Aaron's 36-yard dart to Jared Cook—who kept his tippy-toes in bounds—at Dallas with three seconds left led to a game-winning field goal. The winning streak finally ended in the AFC Championship Game at Atlanta.

On December 3, 2016, Rodgers turned thirty-three. That's old for an NFL player, but superstar quarterbacks often stick around until their late thirties. Rodgers has given no indications of retiring, but when he does, he hopes it's with the Packers.

"You look at two of my favorite players from my sports-watching lifetime: Derek Jeter and Kobe Bryant ... ," Rodgers said. "They stay with the same team, they stick it out ... I think there's a lot to be said about finishing your legacy with one team. It would be nice if I am able to do that."

Packers fans would agree. In the meantime, they hope he's got a few more miracles left in him.

Stats, Honors, and Records

NFL PASSING STATISTICS									
SEA	TEAM	W-L	CMP	ATT	CMP%	YDS	TD	INT	RAT
2005	GB	--	9	16	56.3	65	0	1	39.8
2006	GB	--	6	15	40.0	46	0	0	48.2
2007	GB	--	20	28	71.4	218	1	0	106.0
2008	GB	6–10	341	536	63.6	4,038	28	13	93.8
2009	GB	11–5	350	541	64.7	4,434	30	7	103.2
2010	GB	10–5	312	475	65.7	3,922	28	11	101.2
2011	GB	14–1	343	502	68.3	4,643	45	6	**122.5**
2012	GB	11–5	371	552	67.2	4,295	39	8	**108.0**
2013	GB	6–3	193	290	66.6	2,536	17	6	104.9
2014	GB	12–4	341	520	65.6	4,381	38	5	112.2
2015	GB	10–6	347	572	60.7	3,821	31	8	92.7
2016	GB	10–6	401	610	65.7	4,428	40	7	104.2
Career	GB	90–45	3,034	4657	65.1	36,827	297	72	104.1

SEA = Season
REC = Record as Starter
CMP = Completions
ATT = Attempts

CMP% = Completion Percentage
YDS = Passing Yards
TD = Touchdown Passes

INT = Interceptions
RAT = Passer Rating
Bold = Led NFL

Major Honors
NFL MVP: 2011, 2014
First Team All-Pro: 2011, 2014
Pro Bowl: 2009, 2011, 2012, 2014, 2015, 2016
Super Bowl MVP: 2010 season

Major NFL Records
104.1 passer rating, career
4.13 touchdown-to-interception ratio, career
1.5 percent interception rate, career
122.5 passer rating, season (2011)

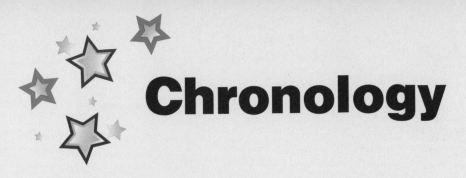

Chronology

December 2, 1983 Aaron Rodgers is born in Chico, California.

2001 season Rodgers breaks the Pleasant Valley High School single-season passing record.

2002 season Earns Junior College All-American honors at Butte College.

2003 season Ends his first season at the University of California with 359- and 394-yard passing games.

2004 season Garners First Team All-Pac-10 honors for Cal.

April 23, 2005 Selected 24th overall by Green Bay in the NFL Draft.

2008 season Becomes the Packers' starting quarterback for the first time.

2009 season Leads Green Bay to an 11–5 record and makes the Pro Bowl.

February 6, 2011 Earns the Super Bowl MVP Award after defeating Pittsburgh 31–25.

2011 Marches the Packers to a 15–1 record, sets the league single-season passer rating record (122.5), and earns NFL MVP honors.

October 14, 2012 Throws six touchdown passes versus Houston.

2012 season Leads the NFL in passer rating (108.0) and makes the Pro Bowl.

September 15, 2013 Ties a team record by throwing for 480 yards against Washington.

December 29, 2013 Throws a last-minute 48-yard TD pass to defeat Chicago and clinch the NFL North Division title.

November 9, 2014 Burns Chicago with six touchdown passes, all in the first half.

2014 season Wins his second NFL MVP Award and leads Green Bay to the NFC Championship Game.

December 3, 2015 Defeats Detroit on a 61-yard Hail Mary pass.

January 22, 2017 Leads the Packers to another NFC Championship Game, but loses to the Atlanta Falcons, 44–21.

Glossary

acumen The ability to quickly and accurately deal with a situation.

All-American Voted one of the best at each position, either at the high school level or the college level; many organizations announce All-American teams.

collarbone Either of the two bones that join the breastbone to the shoulder blades.

completion percentage An equation: passing completions divided by passing attempts.

concussion Damage to the brain caused by a blow to the head.

Division I The top division in the NCAA; there are currently 128 Division I football teams.

First Team All-Pac-10 The best player at each position in the Pacific-10 Conference, as selected by a committee.

gunslinger An aggressive quarterback who frequently throws downfield.

"Hail Mary" pass A long, desperate pass toward the end zone on the last play of the game or half.

interception rate An equation: interceptions divided by passing attempts.

Motown Detroit's nickname; refers to a genre of music produced in that city during the 1960s.

NFL scout A person who evaluates college football players.

passer rating A complicated formula meant to rate a quarterback's passing success; it factors in completions, completion percentage, passing yards, touchdown throws, and interceptions.

recruiter A college coach or other school member who tries to get high school players to come to the school.

scholarship An amount of money that a school gives to a student for education.

wildcard team A nondivision winner that makes the NFL playoffs.

Further Reading

Books

Aretha, David. *Top 10 Quarterbacks in Football.* New York, NY: Enslow Publishing, 2017.

Frederick, Shane. *Side-By-Side Football Stars: Comparing Pro Football's Greatest Players.* North Mankato, MN: Capstone, 2015.

Kelley, K. C. *Quarterback Superstars 2015.* New York, NY: Scholastic Book Service, 2015.

Myers, Dan. *Green Bay Packers.* Edina, MN: ABDO Publishing, 2017.

Websites

Green Bay Packers

packers.com

Includes team news, game coverage, Fan Zone, and bios of players—including Aaron Rodgers.

NFL Zone

sikids.com/nfl-zone

Features lots of fun stories and games centered around the NFL.

Pro Football Reference

pro-football-reference.com

Search "Aaron Rodgers" to find career, season, and game stats on the Packers star.

Index